# LMSR LOCOMOTIVES

## 1923-1948

volume I

## H. C. CASSERLEY

# D. BRADFORD BARTON LIMITED

**Frontispiece:** The original 'Coronation' Pacific, No.6220 *Coronation* herself, after being de-streamlined, passing Northchurch (near Berkhamsted) with the down 'Royal Scot' during the great freeze of March 1947. These fine engines, together with their predecessors the 'Princesses' and the later 'Duchesses', which were unstreamlined from the outset, represented—along with Gresley's well-known A4s of the LNER—the ultimate achievement of main line express motive power in this country. It is fortunate that examples of both have survived for preservation, some of them in working order, for the benefit of succeeding generations of railway enthusiasts.

© copyright D. Bradford Barton 1976 ☐ ISBN 0 85153 264 0 ☐ Set in Monotype Bembo and printed by offset litho by H. E. Warne Ltd, of London and St. Austell, for the publishers D. Bradford Barton Ltd, of Trethellan House, Truro, Cornwall

# introduction

The 1923 grouping resulting from the 1921 Railways Act made the LMS by far the most important of the four new companies. During the previous year, the London & North Western and the Lancashire & Yorkshire, two of the main constituents, had already amalgamated, forming the largest company in the British Isles, although with no outward visible effect, as for practical purposes the two railways continued their independence until both became part of the new entity.

The LMS inherited 3336 locomotives from the London & North Western, 1668 from the Lancashire & Yorkshire (including 18 steam rail motors), 3019 from the Midland, 1070 from the Caledonian, 528 from the Glasgow & South Western, 173 from the Highland, 192 from the North Stafford, 136 from the Furness, and a handful of others from such small concerns as the Stratford-on-Avon & Midland Junction, Wirral, Maryport & Carlisle, Cleator & Workington, and the Garstang & Knott End. This huge total can be broken down in an interesting manner by quoting a few individual types of wheel arrangement, with such examples as 43 4-2-2 express single wheelers, the last of their kind, of which 42 came from the Midland; 40 Atlantics, all L & YR; and no less than 3423 0-6-0 tender engines, of which nearly half had been owned by the MR. This railway had concentrated on comparatively few types and with one notable exception (the 0-6-0T, of which the GWR had a far greater number) had a larger number of every wheel arrangement than any other railway, ranging from 254 2-4-0s, 386 4-4-0s, 1570 0-6-0 tender engines, down to one 0-10-0, but even this still the maximum! Taking the LMS as a whole, in the light of later

developments, it is interesting to note that in 1923 it had only sixteen 2-6-0s, and but two 2-6-4Ts (and these were only narrow gauge engines on the Leek & Manifold), both of them types which were to be multiplied in large numbers in the ensuing decade. Another ten years were to elapse before the appearance of the first Pacific, a design which had made its initial appearance on the LNER just prior to the grouping—apart from the 'Great Bear' of the GWR of 1908, never multiplied.

The whole locomotive stock was steam, with the exception of one electric and three battery locomotives; the diesel had not yet begun to rear its head, although it was to be the LMS which pioneered this new form of motive power, destined eventually, together with electrification, to oust steam completely as the normal motive power of the foreseeable future.

One of the first considerations affecting the locomotive stock was the question of renumbering, to avoid inevitable confusion. The Midland had had the best and most methodical method since 1907, when it had replaced its previous haphazard numbering list which had grown up through the years by filling in gaps as they happened to occur, and which was still largely the practice with the other constituents, particularly the LNWR and L & YR, brought about by giving a new locomotive any number which happened to be vacant at the time. Under the new system, the passenger tender engines came first, all numbered in separate blocks, the oldest coming first, rising to the newer and more powerful. Passenger tank engines followed, again in ascending order; then goods and shunting tanks, finishing with main line freight engines. The MR engines were unaltered, and after

1923 occupied the number range extending from 1 to 4999, allowing ample room for new construction, the LNWR following with a block allocation 5000 to 9999. The L & YR then came with numbers 10000–13999 and finally the Scottish railways were grouped together under the same pattern, passenger tender engines in the 14000s, passenger tanks 15000s, goods tanks 16000s, goods tender 17000s. The smaller English companies' locomotives were absorbed into suitable places in the three main blocks, 1–4999, 5000–9999 and 10000–12999, and new construction took an appropriate place within any of the four ranges. By the 1930s it was considered desirable to arrange that only four-figure numbers were allocated to standard designs. The survivors of some older classes, which were by then thinning out, had 20000 added to their numbers to clear the way for a complete consecutive run for new engines and renumbering of existing standard classes where they had five-figure numbers.

The first Chief Mechanical Engineer of the LMS was George Hughes from the L & YR, but he did little in the way of new designs except for a 2-6-0 mixed traffic engine. In 1926 he was succeeded by Sir Henry Fowler, from the Midland, who, in addition to introducing new designs, also adopted several existing MR types as standard for further construction—much to the annoyance of the LNWR, always rivals of the Midland. In 1931, Fowler was replaced for a short time by Sir Ernest Lemon, but this was in name only, as he was not a locomotive man and introduced nothing new. The real revolution came in 1932, when Sir William Stanier came over from the Great Western. The 'small engine' policy of the MR came to an abrupt end with the introduction of his well known Pacifics, and many other notable designs. Stanier was in office until 1944, when he was succeeded by C E Fairburn, who was there for only a year when he was replaced in turn by H G Ivatt, son of H A Ivatt, for many years CME of the Great Northern, and best remembered by his Atlantics on that railway. H G Ivatt was destined to be the last CME of the LMS.

The livery adopted at the grouping was the lovely Midland crimson lake, at first for all passenger types, although only nominally as far as the LNWR was concerned, as Crewe was extremely annoyed at the indignity of having to adopt the colours of its old rival, and in fact not many engines other than the Claughtons ever received it; most of the others were turned out in plain black. More than that, they did not approve of the renumbering scheme, and for several years many engines still carried the old LNWR number plates.

In 1928 the decision was made that only the top link express engines would qualify for red livery. For the time being this included only the 'Royal Scots', LNWR 'Claughtons', the Horwich 4-6-0s, and the Midland compounds, of which there were at that time 235 in traffic (only five more of a final batch of 25 in 1932 were actually built, as Sir William Stanier cancelled the order for the rest). At the same time the large engine numbers on the tender were transferred to the cab sides, owing to confusion in identification when one locomotive borrowed the tender of another for some reason. Later the crimson lake was, of course, applied to other new designs until the war years, when all engines succumbed to plain black, Pacifics included, with deplorable maintenance, which never recovered pre-war standards.

This, very briefly, is an outline of the story of the LMS locomotive stock during its twenty-five years of existence. Amongst the several hundred types which were to be seen during that period, it is possible to illustrate only a few, and selection has been made rather—although not entirely—in favour of the older and more unusual types, now only remembered by the older generation of railway enthusiasts; this avoids too much repetition of more modern classes, some of which were familiar during the last days of steam.

The oldest locomotive to come into LMS stock at the 1923 Grouping was this ancient Kirtley 0-6-0WT dating back to 1848, when it was built by the firm of Messrs. E. B. Wilson & Co. Originally No.201 (and later 201A and 1601 at the 1907 renumbering), it became 1605 at the Grouping and was broken up in January 1924.

F. W. Webb's Dx Class from the LNWR, the first of which appeared from Crewe Works in 1858, were built in very large numbers, one of the earliest examples of standardisation on a considerable scale. Several lasted into the Grouping era, including No.8015, late LNWR No.3008, built in 1868, which was withdrawn in December 1927.

Matthew Kirtley on the Midland also concentrated on standardisation at an early date, and built his double-framed 0-6-0 goods engines in large numbers. One of the earliest still in existence upon withdrawal in 1925 had been built by Kitson Thompson & Hewitson in 1856. It was set aside, together with several other engines, for preservation, and given its original number 421. It is seen here at Derby in June 1929, outside the paint shop, where these relics were stored. Unfortunately, when (Sir) William Stanier came on the scene in 1932, all were ruthlessly cut up with one exception, the Johnson single, which was fortunately spared.

Another very old engine was this crane tank of the North London Railway, built by Sharp Stewart in 1858 for the North & South Western Junction Railway, originally as a 0-4-0ST. It was converted to its later form at Bow Works in 1872. Formerly NLR No.29, then 29A, it eventually became LNWR 2896, LMS 7217, later 27217, and even survived Nationalisation to appear as BR No.58865. It was withdrawn from service in 1951 and sent to Derby for possible preservation, but unfortunately this did not materialise.

A scene in Derby paint shop, June 1926. In the foreground is No.3, a double-framed Kirtley 2-4-0, which had emerged from the famous works back in 1866. Of another long-lived class, this one, originally numbered 159 and later 159A until 1907, was scrapped in 1928. The first of them, No.1 (see page 65), was one of the small group of engines already mentioned on page 8, set aside for preservation, but later broken up. However, No.2, ultimately 20002, the last to remain in traffic, was secured on withdrawal in 1947, and restored to its earlier condition as MR 158A. After being housed for several years in a museum at Leicester, it is now destined to return to Derby under the auspices of the Midland Railway Company preservation society. The other engine in the photograph is a Johnson 4-4-0 rebuilt by Deeley, No.562.

William Stroudley, best known for his achievements as Locomotive Superintendent of the London Brighton & South Coast Railway, started his career on the Highland where he occupied a similar position from 1866–1869. During this period he designed three small 0-6-0Ts, the direct antecedents of his much better known 'Terriers' on the LB & SCR. All lasted until LMS days, the earliest of them, formerly HR No.56B *Dornoch*, is seen here at Inverness as LMS No.16118 in June 1927. It was scrapped later the same year.

Another early standard LNWR type, built by F. W. Webb, were his 0-6-0STs, or 'Special Tanks' as they were usually ca No.7298, late LNWR No.3580, built in 1873, here seen shunting at Chester in June 1932, had only a few months to go b withdrawal. Most of the class had disappeared by World War II, but a small handful survived as works shunters at Crewe Wolverton Carriage Works until the 1950s.

'Dignity and Impudence' Derby, June 1928. Another veteran Kirtley engine, 0-4-4T No.1200, built by Beyer Peacock in 1869, faces up to newly constructed 'Royal Scot' No.6141 *Caledonian* (later renamed *The North Staffordshire Regiment*). These 'Royal Scots', at first perpetuating the names of much older locomotives, carried beautifully engraved etchings on a brass plate mounted beneath the nameplate itself, as in the illustration of *Samson* (No.6135) but these were later removed when the class received regimental names.

The only surviving 2-4-0 from the Lancashire & Yorkshire Railway was No. 10000, late No.731, built in 1873 to the designs of J. Ramsbottom of the LNWR, and in fact actually constructed at Crewe. Latterly in use on engineers' inspection duties, it was withdrawn in July 1926.

The first engines to be repainted in Midland red, which after 1923 became the standard livery for all passenger classes, bore the initials LMS as in the illustration above, but these were soon replaced by a very fine coat of arms which embodied the crest of the new company organisation. At the same time, fresh works plates were cast. The new administration seemed, for some reason, to wish to eradicate the memory of the constituent companies as quickly as possible, which resulted in such absurdities as these two examples shown, on Midland 0-4-4T No.1259 and Highland 4-4-0 No.14409; both bear inappropriate legends appertaining to many years previous, before the LMS had even been envisaged.

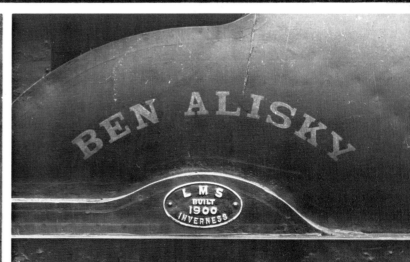

A North London 4-4-0T, the standard class which worked its suburban services for a period of many years until supplanted by newer types after the Grouping—notably LMS 'Jinties' and Stanier 2-6-2 tanks. Although the two railways were very far apart and had nothing in common, the striking similarity between this NLR 4-4-0T, No.6445, and the HR one opposite, cannot fail to be noted. This was another of the several engines set aside for preservation by the LMSR, as already referred to on pages 8 and 10, which were unfortunately consigned to the scrap heap. It is seen here at Derby in June 1929.

A Highland 4-4-0T repainted in Midland colours at Inverness in June 1927. This was one of three built at Lochgorm works in 1878 to the design of David Jones, all of which lasted until 1928-1932.

**Overleaf:** The express single-wheeler was an almost extinct species at the time of the Grouping; there remained only half a dozen on the Great Central, a handful of the once magnificent fleet of ninety-five Johnson 'spinners', and the solitary Caledonian example. This view, taken at Kentish Town in May 1924, shows one of the few of the Midland ones which survived to assume LMS identity, in this case in the first lettering style with new initials on the cabside. No.665 was built at Derby in 1896 as No.75, and ran until 1926. Nearly all of the survivors had gone by 1928, and the last of all, No.673, has fortunately been preserved. Even the strictly utilitarian and down-to-earth William Stanier apparently had not the heart to destroy such a lovely piece of Victoriana. It is perhaps a small consolation to reflect that none of these engines lasted to suffer the indignity of assuming sombre black livery, as they undoubtedly would have done after the general introduction of this in 1928 for all but top link express locomotives.

The remaining representative of the 4-2-2 type was the famous Caledonian No.123, built by Neilson in 1886. It was fortunately preserved at St. Rollox following withdrawal in 1935 and restored to CR blue livery. As is well known, this engine was put back into running order in the late 1950s and worked enthusiasts' specials all over the country for several years before going to a final resting place in Glasgow Museum. It is seen here at Balornock in May 1928, at which time it was used solely on working the directors' saloon, although it later finished its normal career on local trains between Perth and Dundee.

Matthew Kirtley's earlier express engines for the Midland consisted of a series of 48 double-framed 2-4-0s built in 1870/1, known as the '800' class. Nearly all of them passed out of service during the 1920s, but one, No.60, managed to survive several years after the others, until 1936. This was long enough, in fact, for it to be renumbered into the 20000 'duplicate list' as No.20060. It finished its days working between Leicester and Peterborough, and is seen here at Manton in April 1935.

Crewe did not take kindly to the idea of adopting the red livery of its old rival the Midland, and in fact very few engines, apart from the 'Claughtons', ever received it. Since Webb's typically autocratic edict back in the 1880s—'You can paint them any colour you like, so long as it's black!'—so it had been, and so it remained after the Grouping as far as possible. Here, however, is one of the few exceptions, Webb 2-4-2 No.6741, formerly LNWR No.1386, at an unknown location, about 1924.

The various absorbed Scottish lines, however, co-operated fully in applying the crimson lake, and Caledonian 0-4-4T No. 15222, seen here at Dundee in May 1930, is still in that colour, although a little faded. By this time black had become the official livery for all repaints as engines went through the shops.

4-4-0T No. 15027, also at Dundee on station pilot duty in July 1931, is in black livery with LMS panel on the bunker. This was normally only used on freight and shunting engines, the latter category being then apparently applied to this particular class.

No railway benefited more than the Highland from the LMS crimson lake during the very few years when this was applied to all passenger engines, as is shown by the resplendent appearance of this 0-4-4T, photographed at Dingwall in May 1928. A great pity that colour photography was unknown in a practicable form in those days! What a magnificent illustration this would have made! After 1928, however, no Highland engines, or even newer LMS types introduced to the system, qualified for the express livery and all were relegated to black. Whether by coincidence or otherwise, this was about the time when the high standard of appearance began to deteriorate, culminating eventually through the war years to the deplorable lack of sufficient cleaning and maintenance which eventually became commonplace during the last years of steam.

26

As already mentioned, the LNWR not only objected to crimson lake livery, but they did not like smokebox number plates—probably just because it was a Midland idea! They were fitted in the earlier years in a somewhat half-hearted fashion, but were more often than not removed on the next visit to Crewe. Webb 4ft. 10in. 0-6-2T No.7645 still had one in position at Bletchley in March 1932.

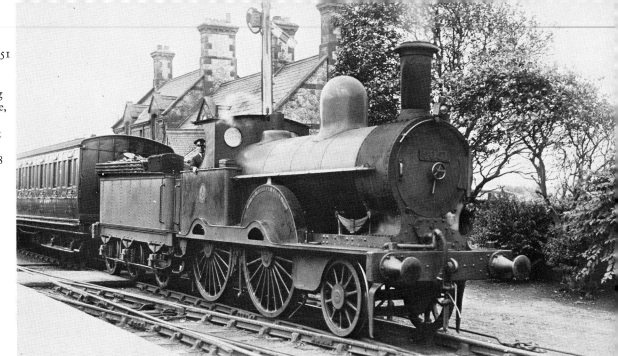

'Precedent' 2-4-0 No.5051 *Sir Hardman Earle*, in black livery but with LMS crest and carrying smokebox number plate, probably on the Cockermouth, Keswick & Penrith line in the late 1920s, prior to 1928 when this engine was scrapped.

Nearly all of Webb's notorious compounds had either been scrapped or converted to simples by the time of the Grouping, but a few 2-8-0s and 0-8-0s survived as such into LMS days; No.9601 (built at Crewe in 1902 as LNWR No.905) at an unknown location somewhere between renumbering in November 1926 and July 1928, when it was scrapped.

The Stratford-on-Avon & Midland Junction was one of the minor systems absorbed into the LMS, its long straggling cross-country line through Bedford, Northants and Warwick being now entirely closed. Its small stock of about eighteen locomotives consisted very largely of a miscellaneous collection of 0-6-0s. One of these, No.2305, formerly SMJ 11, built by Beyer Peacock in 1896 and scrapped in 1930, is seen at Derby in 1926.

A pair of Kirtley's numerous double-framed 0-6-0s, Nos.2533 and 2538, at Toton in June 1928, preparing to leave the shed to work a freight train on the Erewash Valley line, a common sight in those days. Many of the class lasted well into the 1930s, when they were to be found on most parts of the system, although after World War I they were rarely to be seen south of Wellingborough.

Amongst the less unusual Highland Railway classes were some 0-6-0s designed by Peter Drummond and built by Dübs & Co in 1902. They were almost indistinguishable from a much more numerous series built by his brother Dugald on the Caledonian during the 1880s. One of the HR engines is seen here at Corkerhill in April 1948 in company with rebuilt 'Royal Scot' No.6103 *Royal Scots Fusilier*.

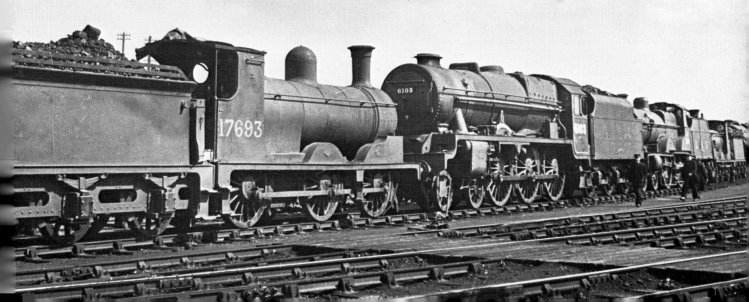

Most of Johnson's earlier classes of 4-4-0 for express working on the Midland—that is, prior to the large Belpaires introduced in 1900, followed by the compounds—were found to be somewhat underboilered, and nearly all were later completely reconstructed by Deeley and Fowler to a degree in which they were in fact practically new engines. The original 30 however, which dated back to 1876–77, were never rebuilt and remained virtually in their original condition to the end. Some of these had been scrapped as early as 1911–12, but about half were still at work at the Grouping. One of the last survivors, No.320, repainted with LMS crest, made what was by that time a rare appearance in London as late as September 1926, piloting an up express, and was photographed at Kentish Town shed on that occasion. This particular one was scrapped in 1928, but the last survivor of all, No.311, survived until 1934. A later No. 320 will be found on page 73.

Concurrently with the 4-4-0s mentioned opposite, Johnson also built large numbers of very similar 2-4-0s until 1881, after which he decided on the 4-4-0 wheel arrangement, although of course he also returned to the single-wheeler for express working. The 2-4-0s were again of several varieties, the main difference being in the size of driving wheels, which ranged between 6ft. 3in. and 7ft. One of the latter, rebuilt with Belpaire firebox—a modification which was applied to a considerable number of these 2-4-0s in later years, as well as to other Johnson classes (although none of the 4-4-0s ever received this treatment)—is seen here at Peterborough (East) with a train for Nottingham in May 1937. No.204 became No.20204 in 1936 under a partial renumbering scheme introduced two years earlier to clear complete blocks of numbers, still partly occupied by survivors of older classes, to allow for new construction. This was done by the simple expedient of adding 20000 and was in effect the re-creation of the principle of the old time duplicate list formerly adopted by many of the old companies, usually by the addition of a suffix 'A' or some other similar method.

No.14236, an old Glasgow & South Western 4-4-0, was built at Kilmarnock in 1876 to the design of James Stirling, brother of the better known Patrick, who had preceded him on the G & S WR but who later became famous on the Great Northern. An idiosyncrasy shared not only by these two brothers, but also a third, Matthew (one time locomotive superintendent on the Hull & Barnsley) was the invariable use of domeless boilers, the normal position of the dome being either occupied by the safety valve, as with this engine, or by nothing at all. James Stirling also continued the tradition after he left the G & S WR in 1877, when he went to the South Eastern, for which railway he built some very similar engines to the one depicted here. No.14236, photographed at Hurlford in May 1928, was scrapped in 1930.

No.17066, another G & S W R Stirling engine, built by Neilson & Co in 1876, also originally had the typical domeless boiler but in this case was rebuilt by one of Stirling's successors with a more orthodox domed type. This photograph was also taken at Hurlford in May 1928.

The Caledonian had several classes of 4-6-0s, for the most part in small numbers, and the earlier ones of these were of the inside cylinder variety. No.14607 is seen here at Oban in June 1927. This was one of a class of nine with driving wheels of only 5ft. diameter, built in 1902 and 1905 specially for working over the severely graded Callander and Oban line. They did good work over this difficult road until supplanted by more modern classes in the 1930s, and were a rare instance of an individual class of engine being built especially for working over a particularly difficult line. Prior to their introduction, there had also been several small 4-4-0s known as the 'Oban Bogies' (see page 41) for the same duties, whilst there were the 'Skye Bogies' for the Kyle of Lochalsh line, and the 'West Highland Bogies' of the North British.

The best remembered 4-6-0s of the CR were the 'Cardean' class, one of which is seen here at Larbert in May 1928 piloted by Dunalastair 4-4-0 No.14457 on an express for Glasgow.

As is now widely known, the Highland was responsible for the introduction by David Jones of the 4-6-0 type to Great Britain. Fifteen of them, known as the 'Jones goods', appeared in 1894, including this example, No.17922, seen at Perth in May 1928. The original engine, HR 103, has been preserved and is to be seen in Glasgow Museum.

LNWR Whale 'Precursor' No.5236 *Watt* at Stafford in July 1933. These engines, introduced in 1904, revolutionised main line working on the LNWR, which had hitherto to rely mainly on the uncertainties of the various Webb compounds, supplemented by the gallant efforts of his small but far more reliable 'Precedent' 2-4-0s (see page 29). The 'Precursors' were followed by the even more efficient superheated version, the 'George the Fifth' class, in 1910. All had almost disappeared by World War II, but a few lingered on, including two or three just into BR days after Nationalisation in 1948.

One of the distinctive L & YR Atlantics, No.10303, sometimes known as 'Highflyers', and almost unique for this wheel arrangement in having inside cylinders. These were built around the turn of the century, but had all gone by the early 1930s.

The North Stafford, one of the smaller lines which came into the LMS orbit, possessed five 4-4-0s for express working. At first numbered 595–599 in the Midland series, they were renumbered 5410–5414 in the LNWR block in 1928, consequent on building the further MR type Class 2s for which their numbers were required. All, however, were withdrawn very shortly afterwards, except No.5413, which lasted until 1933.

Two Glasgow & South Western 4-4-0s at Hurlford in May 1928, of a class built at Kilmarnock in 1904 to the design of James Manson. Note the rather unusual bogie tender of the second engine. Both of these engines were scrapped in the early 1930s and in fact G & S W R fared by far the worst amongst the major companies as a result of the Grouping. All but a few of its 529 engines which came into the hands of the L M S had gone by 1939.

Caledonian 'Oban Bogie' No.14103, a class already referred to on page 36. Built by Dübs & Co in 1882 and scrapped in 1930, it was photographed at Stirling in May 1928.

Stalwarts of the Highland; 'Loch' Class No.14386 *Loch Tummel* and 'Castle' No.14681 *Skibo Castle* outside Wick shed in May 1928. These engines, above all others, were the mainstay of passenger working on the long and difficult Highland road from about the turn of the century. The 'Lochs' were the design of David Jones, and the 'Castles' of his successor, Peter Drummond. Fifteen of the former came out in 1896, followed by fifteen 'Castles' which appeared between 1900 and 1913; between them, together with the Jones goods already referred to, they were the backbone of the HR locomotive stock until and during the first World War. When new engines were urgently required in 1917, three more of each class were obtained from the North British Locomotive Company, reliance being placed on these elderly and dependendable types rather than a more modern but untried design. The last 'Castle' went in 1946, but one 'Loch' managed to survive Nationalisation, being withdrawn in March 1948.

The 0-6-4T has never been a widely used wheel arrangement and, although a few examples were to be found on all four groups, it saw more service on the LMS than on any of the others. The Midland, as usual with any of the more restricted range of types than other railways, had the largest number. Even so this totalled only forty, all built at Derby in 1907. Unfortunately this was one of the few really unsatisfactory designs on the MR. Designed by R.M. Deeley, they were intended for suburban passenger work; their somewhat ungainly appearance, partly due to the extended side tanks which earned for them the not inappropriate nickname of 'flatirons', was not entirely negatived by their actual performance. They worked mostly on suburban services in the Birmingham and Manchester districts but a few later found their way to the London area. They were however undoubtedly somewhat clumsy machines, and following some derailments in the 1930s they were confined to local freight work; all had gone by 1938. Originally unsuperheated, they were later rebuilt with super-heaters, extended smokeboxes and Belpaire fireboxes, as in the illustration of No.2014, at Derby in July 1928.

The North Stafford had small numbers of two classes of 0-6-4Ts, with 5ft. driving wheels, mainly used on freight work, and with 5ft. 6in. intended for passenger duties; one of the former, painted in red passenger livery is seen at Stoke-on-Trent in 1932.

The Highland also possessed eight 0-6-4Ts, mainly used on banking duties. No.15304 at Blair Atholl in July 1931, was photographed shortly before assisting a north-bound train up to Druimuchdar, at 1484ft. above sea level Britain's highest main line summit.

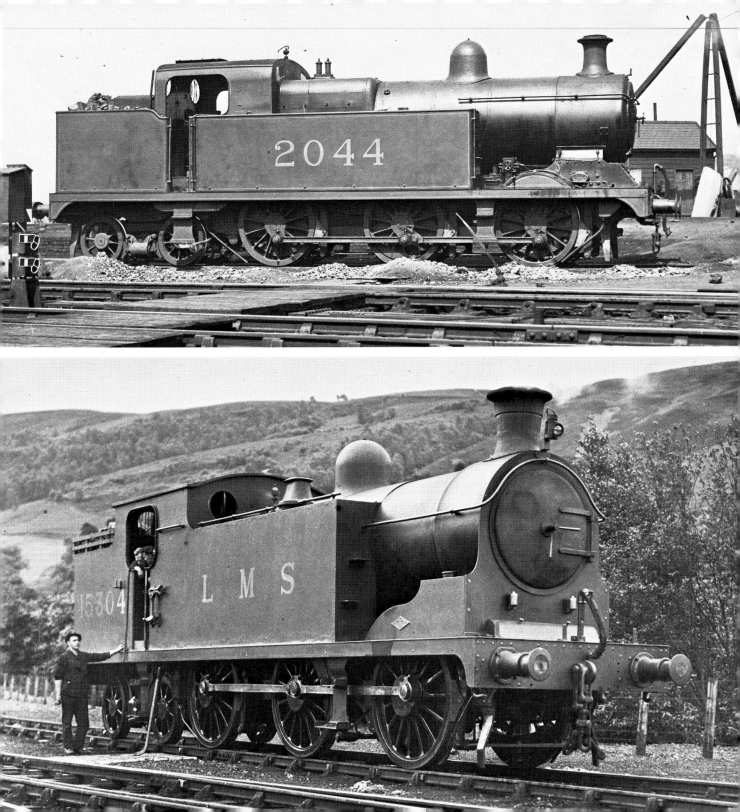

The 4-6-4T type, or 'Baltic tank', was another design not widely used in Britain, again being found only in very small numbers, on four pregrouping railways, three of which came into the LMS. There were also the LMS-built Horwich engines mentioned on page 55. R.H. Whitelegg, locomotive superintendent of the London Tilbury & Southend when that railway was absorbed by the Midland in 1912, had eight large 4-6-4Ts under construction for the line's busy suburban service, and these came straight into the Midland stock as Nos.2100–2107. As it turned out, they were never of much use on the line, as their weight prohibited them from running into Fenchurch Street, and they were eventually transferred to the Midland system itself, on some suburban workings out of St. Pancras, but mainly on freight trains between Wellingborough and Cricklewood. No.2100 is seen at Plaistow in August 1925; all eight in the class disappeared between 1929 and 1934.

Whitelegg later became locomotive superintendent of the G & S W R, for which railway he brought out six very similar engines for the express service between Glasgow and Ayr, Nos.15400 to 15405, built in 1922. They were excellent machines but, as with many other numerically small non-standard types, they had short lives and were withdrawn in 1935–36.

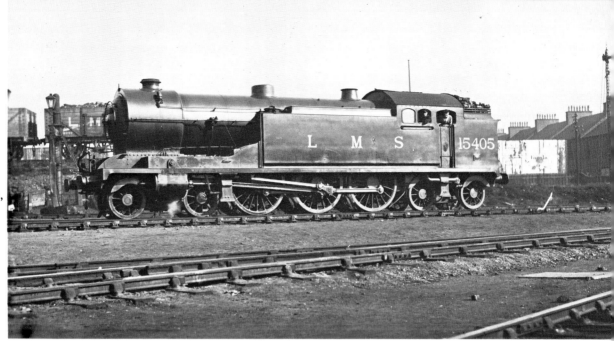

The Furness also had four 4-6-4Ts, this time with inside cylinders, Nos.11100–11104, built in 1920. These also were destined for early extinction, all having gone by 1940; No.11102 with a Whitehaven train leaving Carnforth about 1925.

The LNWR's principal main line freight type was the 0-8-0, of which the earliest examples had been built in the 1890s as three- and four-cylinder compounds by F. W. Webb. These were all eventually either scrapped or converted to two-cylinder simples, in which form the type was multiplied in considerable numbers by Bowen-Cooke from 1910 onwards, culminating in the superheated G2 Class which came out from Crewe in 1921–22. One of them, No.9411, is seen here at Addison Road on the West London line, on a through freight train from the Southern system to Willesden Junction in August 1933.

The CR and G & SWR each had a small number of 2-6-0s, both designs being—very unusually for this type—inside cylinder machines. The Caledonian ones, five in number (Nos.17800–17804) were built in 1912, and the eleven G & SWR (Nos.17820–17830) in 1915. No.17801 was photographed at Kingmoor in August 1931, and No.17830 at Corkerhill in May 1928. Nearly all had been withdrawn by the mid-1930s, but three of the G & SWR batch lasted into the war years, when they saw service on the far north road of the Highland.

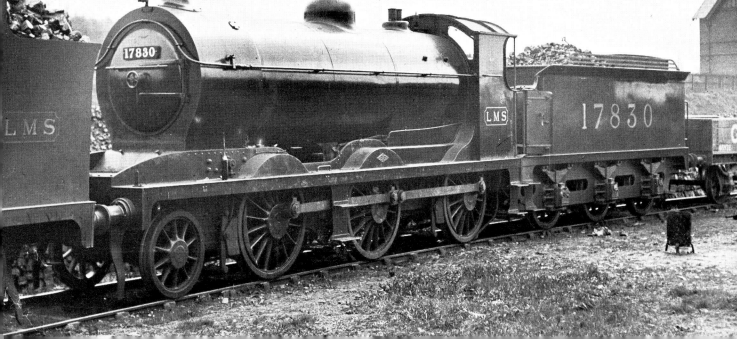

Two Midland 0-4-0Ts at Staveley in June 1936. There were ten of these, mostly used in dock areas, collieries and the like. Note the inconsistency in the arrangement of the numerals and LMS lettering on these two locomotives. Incidentally these tanks were extremely rare as far as Midland engines were concerned in having outside cylinders. Apparently the only other examples since the very earliest days were the three-cylinder compounds, the solitary four-cylinder 0-10-0 Lickey banker, an 0-6-0ST acquired from

the Severn & Wye in 1895, and the 2-6-0s imported from the USA in 1899—hardly surprising in this case, as they were of American design. There was also at one time a set of six 4-4-0Ts of Beyer Peacock design, and one must not overlook the numerous 4-4-2Ts and the 4-6-4Ts inherited from the LT & SR in 1912, although none of these were true Midland engines.

Locomotives from four small railways which came into the LMS at the Grouping; No.6762, originally an L & YR engine, was sold to the Wirral Railway in 1921, and was consequently included amongst the miscellaneous collection of locomotives acquired from that company, most of which were scrapped very soon without acquiring their newly allocated LMS numbers (mostly odd gaps in the 6700s, 6800s and 6900s). This one, however, survived the others by many years, and in fact lasted to become BR No.46762, and was not withdrawn until 1952.

An old Maryport & Carlisle Railway 0-6-0, No. 12484, built in 1875 and scrapped in 1930; photographed at Carlisle in August 1926.

The five engines acquired by the LMS from the Cleator & Workington Railway were all 0-6-0STs, very similar to No.11566 *Hutton Hall* which was built by Peckett and Son in 1907 and scrapped in 1927.

The Garstang & Knott End Railway provided only four additions to the LMS stock, a miscellaneous collection consisting of two 0-6-0STs, a 0-6-0T, also—a very unusual type for this country—a 2-6-0T. This one, No.11680 *Blackpool*, is the engine at the rear of this photograph; in the foreground is *New Century*, allocated No.11301 (but never carried, as it was scrapped in 1925). *Blackpool*, in turn, lasted only until 1927.

George Hughes, of the Lancashire & Yorkshire, was the first locomotive superintendent of the LMS, until succeeded by Sir Henry Fowler, of the Midland, in 1925. For a start he built a further batch of his four-cylinder express 4-6-0s; these came out as LMS Nos.10456–10475 during 1924–5, and were allocated to the North Western Division for the West Coast main line, principally for use between Crewe and Carlisle as substitutes for the never too successful 'Claughtons'. In 1926 Fowler converted No.10456 for compound working, but the experiment was not pursued, and the engine later reverted to simple. No.10462 was photographed at Crewe in June 1929.

At the same time Hughes adapted his 4-6-0 design as a 4-6-4T for use on its native Lancashire & Yorkshire system, where a more powerful engine for express work was needed. With its comparatively short hauls, tank engines were very suitable for much of the L & YR road, and the earlier 2-4-2Ts had indeed been used for many years on subsidiary main line work. These new 4-6-4Ts had been actually ordered prior to the Grouping, and were to have been L & YR Nos.1684–1693. The original intention had been to build twenty, but Nos.1694–1703 in the event appeared as the 4-6-0 version (see opposite), whilst the ten actually constructed as 4-6-4Ts, which were not ready until March 1924, came out as LMS Nos.11110 to 11119.

Although the first of the new LMSR 2-6-0 mixed traffic engines appeared in 1926 under the Fowler regime, this was a design really emanating from Horwich, where it had been planned three years earlier. After sundry second or third thoughts, the class emerged in the form in which it later became well known, under the nickname of 'Crab'. With an extremely high running plate and absence of splashers, the new design presented a revolutionary appearance at the time, but was a direct portent of future fashion. The first thirty engines, Nos. 13000–13029, were all built at Horwich, followed by another sixty, Nos. 13040–13099, from Crewe in 1926–7; all of these came out in LMS crimson lake, but the remainder, Nos. 13100–13244, were in black livery. Nos.13100 to 13109 went new to the Highland, where they did excellent work until superseded by the ubiquitous 'Black Fives'. The original, No. 13000, has been preserved. No. 13004, when photographed at Carnforth in July 1932, was still in red livery.

The well known Midland compound design, originally introduced by Johnson in 1901 and modified by Deeley in 1905, totalled 45 engines by 1909, after which no more were built by the MR. The design was, however, adopted after the Grouping by Sir Henry Fowler as a standard type for future construction, the only slight modification being in the use of 6ft. 9in. coupled wheels in place of 7ft. No less than 190 of them were built between 1924 and 1927; one of the 1927 batch, No.923, built by the Vulcan Foundry, is seen at Perth in May 1930. A further order for another 25 was commenced in 1932, but only five had been built when Stanier came on the scene and, with his very different ideas, cancelled the order for the rest, which would have been Nos.940–959. The complete range, including the original Midlands, embraced the numbers 1000–1199 and 900–939, as the numbers from 1200 were already filled by 0-4-4Ts.

Another Midland type adopted as standard for new construction was the smaller Class 2 4-4-0, intended for intermediate passenger work. These were slightly modified in the same way as the compounds by the substitution of 6ft. 9in. driving wheels in place of 7ft. Many of them went to the G & S W R section in Scotland, where they soon ousted the older types of 4-4-0s, which very soon found their way to the scrap heap in consequence. No.645 is seen here at Portpatrick in June 1937.

Although not adopted as a general standard type in the strictest sense, further examples of the LT & SR design were built after the grouping between 1923 and 1930, to comply with the particular requirements of that line. No.2111 is seen at Plaistow in September 1931, together with one of the original and very much smaller versions, No.2080, which dated back to 1880.

The London Tilbury & Southend had always relied almost entirely on 4-4-2 tanks for its busy suburban services; one of these, No.2157, is seen here at Plaistow in August 1925, at that date still in unsuperheated condition.

The Class 4 goods, first introduced by Fowler in 1911, was another class adopted as standard and built in large numbers. The Midland already had 192 of them by the Grouping (Nos.3835 to 4026) and they followed at intervals right through to 1940, by which time a further 580 had been built (Nos.4027 to 4606), including five originally constructed for the Somerset & Dorset, but which became LMS engines in 1930. They were a good general-purpose engine which could be used on almost any duty, although designed principally for freight work. They were often to be seen on cross-country passenger trains, and even on some expresses, particularly on excursions and holiday reliefs during the summer weekends. The first withdrawals took place in 1954, but many of them remained in service almost to the end of steam. One of the original Midland engines, No.3924, together with No.4027, the first of the LMS-built ones, has been preserved. The illustration shows No.4036 with a local goods at Trent in July 1947.

The two number ones on the LMS, a Kirtley 2-4-0 as running about 1927 and a Fowler 2-6-2T, a new design introduced in 1930 as a standard type. The latter, photographed at Barrow in June 1947, was at first numbered 15500, but became No.1 in May 1934.

The long-felt need for an express passenger tank engine was at last met by Sir Henry Fowler with his 2-6-4Ts, the first of which appeared from Derby in December 1927. There were eventually 125 of them, Nos.2300–2424, and the general design was subsequently adopted by Stanier and continued by his successors Fairburn and Ivatt right through to Nationalisation. The important difference of these later engines was in the employment of a taper boiler (see page 83), whilst some for the Tilbury section had three cylinders in place of two. The illustration shows No.2387 when new at Derby in May 1933. In the rear is 2-6-2T No. 15509 (later No.10), of the class depicted on page 63.

A small semi-standard class consisting of only ten engines, designed by Fowler in 1928 for dock shunting work, successively bore the Nos.11270–11279, 7100–7109, 7160–7169 and eventually BR 47160–47169; No.7167 at Greenock in October 1946.

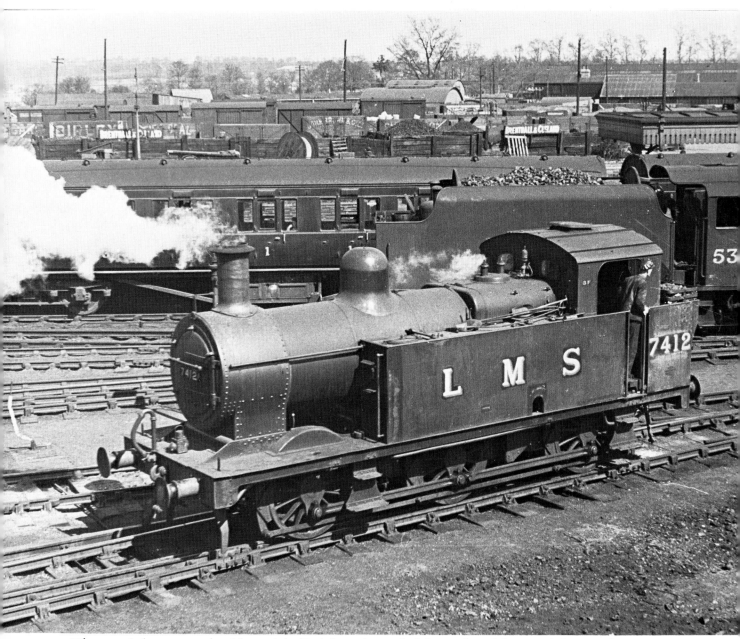

What were in later years to be nicknamed the 'Jinties' was the standard design adopted for general shunting, short distance freight and passenger work, and the like. 422 of them appeared between 1924 and 1931, including some which started life as S&DJR engines. Originally numbered from 7100 to 7149 and 16400 to 16764, they eventually became 7260 to 7681; No.7412 at Watford in April 1947.

Claughton No.6000, former LNWR No.15 and built in 1920, seen in original condition at Crewe in June 1931.

Several of the Claughtons were nominally rebuilt by Fowler to form the prototype of his 'Patriot' Class, but they were purely replacements, assuming the number and identity of the old locomotives but in fact entirely new. The reincarnated No.6000 is seen at Kentish Town in 1933, when new. Later it became No.5538 and received the name *Giggleswick*.

Further examples of the 1934 renumbering involved certain older classes having 20000 added to their numbers to make way for new construction, as already noted on page 33. One of these was Johnson Midland Class 2 0-6-0 No.22969, rebuilt with Belpaire firebox, Ramsbottom safety valves, and Deeley cab. It will be noted that it still retains the pre-1928 style of painting with large numerals on the tender, and that the extra '2' is an obvious recent addition; Derby, May 1934.

Surviving LNWR engines numbered in the 5000s (except the Claughtons, which started at 5900) were also renumbered to pro a complete range to accommodate the Stanier 'Class fives' and 'Jubilees' then planned to be built on a considerable scale; 'Pr of Wales' Class 4-6-0 No.25638 *Charles James Lever* at Rugby, July 1935.

The Lickey incline 0-10-0, No.2290, later became No.22290 when the building of new 2-6-4Ts began to encroach into this number range; seen here at Bromsgrove as No.22290, in May 1948, prior to banking a train up the incline.

When the S&DJR locomotives were absorbed into LMS stock in 1930, the eleven 2-8-0s received at first the numbers 9670 to 9680. This view shows 9672, late S & DJR 82, at Bath in June 1930. When these numbers were later required for a new class of 0-8-0s (opposite) they were renumbered 13800 to 13810. Subsequently becoming BR 53800 to 53810, they nearly all ran until the early 1960s, and one of them has been preserved. Of obvious Derby design and parentage, it is somewhat strange that the Midland never built any for its own use, although one was tried out for a time between Toton and Cricklewood.

The second LMS No.9672 was one of the final batch of a new type of 0-8-0 introduced by Fowler in 1929, eventually totalling 175 engines, Nos.9500–9674. It will be noted that these again possessed several Midland characteristics, and may be regarded as what an MR 0-8-0 would have looked like if that railway had ever had any. Perhaps it was just as well they did not, as these engines did not come up to expectations or turn out to be an outstanding success; No.9672, fitted with an experimental form of feed water heater, at Wakefield, June 1937.

To provide a larger engine capable of hauling heavy coal trains over the Midland from Toton to Cricklewood and avoid the established practice of double-heading with a couple of 0-6-0s, Sir Henry Fowler ordered three 2-6-6-2 Garratts, from Beyer Peacock, and these commenced work in 1927. They were numbered 4997–4999, the last of these being seen here at Toton in June 1928. They were followed in 1930 by another 30, Nos.4967–4996. In 1939 the whole class became Nos.7967–7999 in consequence of the necessity of numbering new 'Black fives', then on order, back into the later 4000s.

To alleviate the additional work imposed on the fireman, the whole class, with the exception of Nos.4998 and 4999, were later fitted with revolving rotary bunkers. The 'Garratt' never really established itself in this country, as it did abroad, and these were the only ones to appear, apart from the solitary Gresley 2-8-8-2 for the LNER and a few small 0-4-4-0s for industrial use.

The earlier S & DJR 4-4-0s acquired by the LMS in 1930 were given numbers of scrapped Midl engines in the early 300s. No.326, a standard Class 2, and No.320, late S & DJR No.77, one pair of an earlier design built at Derby in 1907, at Bath in June 1930. The original LMS 32 illustrated earlier in the volume, on page 32.

No.6399 *Fury* was an experimental member of the 'Royal Scot' Class, built in 1930. This had a complicated three barrel boiler with varying pressures, the maximum being no less than 900lbs. per sq. in. It ran several trials and on one occasion burst a tube with fatal results to an inspector on the footplate, and never ran in ordinary service. Seen here in Derby paint shop in September 1932, *Fury* was eventually reconstructed with a Stanier taper boiler and became No.6170 *British Legion* which formed the prototype for the eventual rebuilding of the 'Royal Scots'.

Amongst the locomotives acquired from the Somerset & Dorset in 1930 were some old six-coupled saddle tanks dating back to 1874–6, built by Fox Walker & Co. They were mostly used on the north Somerset collieries, including No.1502, late S & DJR No.3, seen at Radstock in June 1930.

The LMS acquired a few narrow gauge systems, amongst which was the 2ft. 6in. gauge Leek & Manifold Light Railway, a subsidiary of the North Stafford, running through beautiful surroundings in North Derbyshire. Mainly a tourist line with a certain amount of milk and other agricultural traffic, this remained open only for thirty years, during

which time it possessed but two engines, a couple of sturdy 2-6-4Ts built by Kitson & Co in 1904, No.1 *E. R. Calthrop* and No.2 *J. B. Earle*. These were never renumbered into LMS stock, although the line remained in operation until 1934. No.2 was photographed at Hulme End, the remote terminus of the railway, in 1933.

One of the last users of the direct-drive steam railcar, tried out by various railways during the first decade of the century, was the Lancashire & Yorkshire, which still had eighteen of these units in service at the time of the Grouping.

No.10616 is seen here in June 1933 at Edlington, terminus of the Dearne Valley line. This particular one was scrapped later in the same year, and nearly all had gone by the end of the 1930s, although one survived until 1948.

A Worsdell von Borries two-cylinder compound 2-4-0, No.52, on the NCC at Belfast in August 1930. This engine was built for the Belfast & Northern Counties Railway in 1892 and acquired its large boiler in 1929 with, it will be noted, a characteristic Midland chimney. The B & NCR had been taken over by the MR in 1903, being known henceforth as the Northern Counties Committee, and as such the railway came into the LMS system at the Grouping. By the 1930s it was a miniature version of the old Midland, even to the crimson lake livery applied to all locomotives—both passenger and goods—and the coaching stock. No.52 was rebuilt as a 4-4-0 simple engine in 1931 and became No.4 *Glengariff*, being finally scrapped in 1949.

After 1923 the NCC engines acquired an increasingly Midland appearance, apart from the red livery, and some n ones were in fact built at Derby. No.83 *Carra Castle*, however, seen at Belfast in April 1948, was a product of North British Locomotive Company in 1925. The LMS crest can be distinctly seen on the cabside.

A new design of 2-6-0 appeared from Derby works in 1933 for NCC express work, again with strong Midla characteristics, although not quite like anything on the parent LMS system. The class eventually totalled fift engines, the last ones being built at Belfast in 1942, where No.91 *The Bush* was photographed in June 1937. Consequ upon dieselisation, all had gone by 1965.

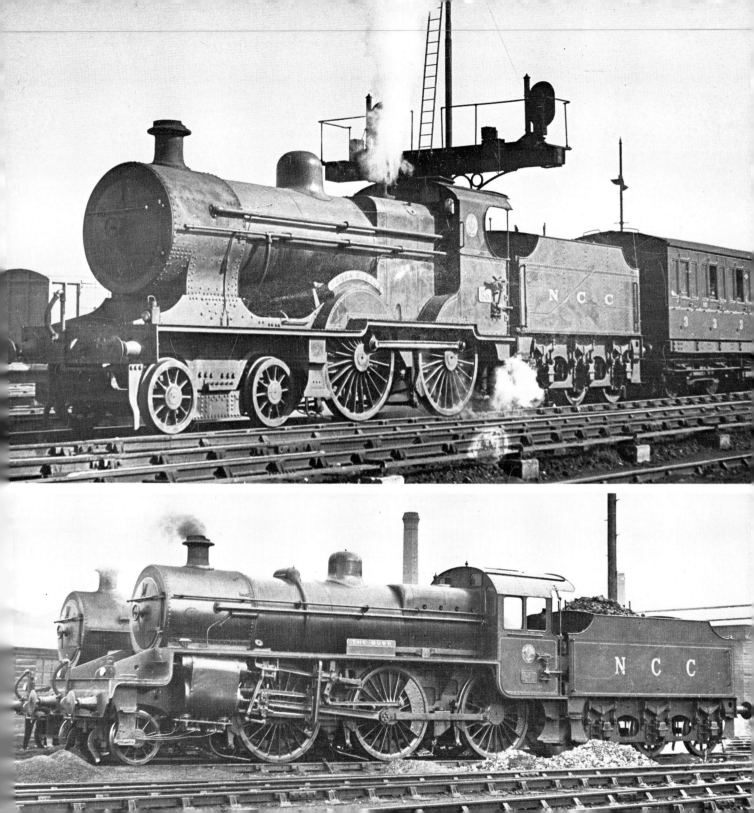

In 1935, after the advent of his well-known Pacifics and 4-6-0s, Stanier introduced a modified version of Fowler's 2-6-2 tanks (see page 63), the chief difference being in his use of a domeless taper boiler. No.111 is seen here new at Derby in July 1935 and, in the rear, one of the 0-4-4Ts, No.6402.

Fowler's 2-6-4T design was also modified by Stanier in the same way but, as with all of his designs, he eventually found it advantageous to revert to the use of a dome. Several hundred of these successful engines were built, and the design was to be adopted with very little alteration as one of the twelve BR standard types in the form of the 80000 Class. No.2222 is seen here on the LT & SR section at Tilbury Docks in May 1947.

The success of the Stanier 'Black Five' is too well known to need recapitulation here beyond mentioning that they were undoubtedly the most useful general purpose steam locomotives this country ever saw, and that no less than 842 of them were built between 1934 and 1950. One of the original engines, as first built with domeless boiler, No.5157 *The Glasgow Highlander*—one of the very few to bear a name—at Inverness about 1936.

Stanier's three-cylinder 'Jubilees' were equally capable locomotives for express work on anything but the heaviest trains and gave particularly good service on the old Midland system right through to the end of steam; No.5622 *Nyasaland* running into Carlisle on a train from Leeds, May 1936.

e of the later ones in the class, No.4924 when new in April 1946. Again on the Highland section, viemore, she is fitted with a snow plough.

A most unusual photograph of the second of the original Stanier Pacifics built in 1933, No.6201 *Princess Elizabeth*, fitted with an experimental double stovepipe chimney, which it carried for only a very short time. This engine is now preserved, as is No.6203 *Princess Margaret Rose*.

[BR Publicity Dept, Euston

The third of the three original Pacifics was built with turbine propulsion in place of normal reciprocating cylinders and valve gear. It ran successfully in this form for many years, being eventually converted to an orthodox four cylinder engine. But as such its life was very short, as it was damaged beyond repair in the disastrous Harrow accident in 1952. Seen here at Crewe in June 1947, on its normal turn, the 8.30 a.m. Euston to Liverpool and 5.25 p.m. return.

e of the first streamlined Pacifics, built in 1937 for working the newly introduced 'Coronation
ot' between Euston and Glasgow, was No.6221 *Queen Elizabeth*, photographed at Polmadie
d in June 1937. Both engines and coaches used on this train were painted in a new livery of blue
h white horizontal bands.

Another of Sir William Stanier's most successful designs was his 2-8-0 freight engine, introduced in 1935, and filling a badly felt gap in the range of LMS motive power. At last the LMS had a good, robust and reliable locomotive capable of handling the heaviest goods traffic. So successful was the design that it was adopted by the War Department as one of the standard types for use during World War II, both at home and overseas. Many hundreds were built, not only in the LMS workshops at Crewe and Horwich, and by outside firms such as Vulcan Foundry and the North British Locomotive Company, but even by the other groups' works such as Swindon, Doncaster, Eastleigh, Brighton and Ashford—an unprecedented occurrence. Some even started life as LNER engines, as in the illustration opposite. No.8048, one of the original lot, with an up freight passing Mill Hill in June 1937.

One of the odd effects of the intermingling of the four groups which occur under wartime conditions is exemplified by the works plate on No.8455, of the batch of 8Fs built at Swindon. This was the shape of things to com anticipating Nationalisation, which actually took place in 1948.

A Stanier 2-8-0 in strange guise;
LNER No.3506 at Colwick, July
1947. The LNER temporarily owned
68 of these engines, Nos.3500–3567 in
their list, but in 1947 they were
transferred to the LMS, becoming
Nos. 8705–8772.

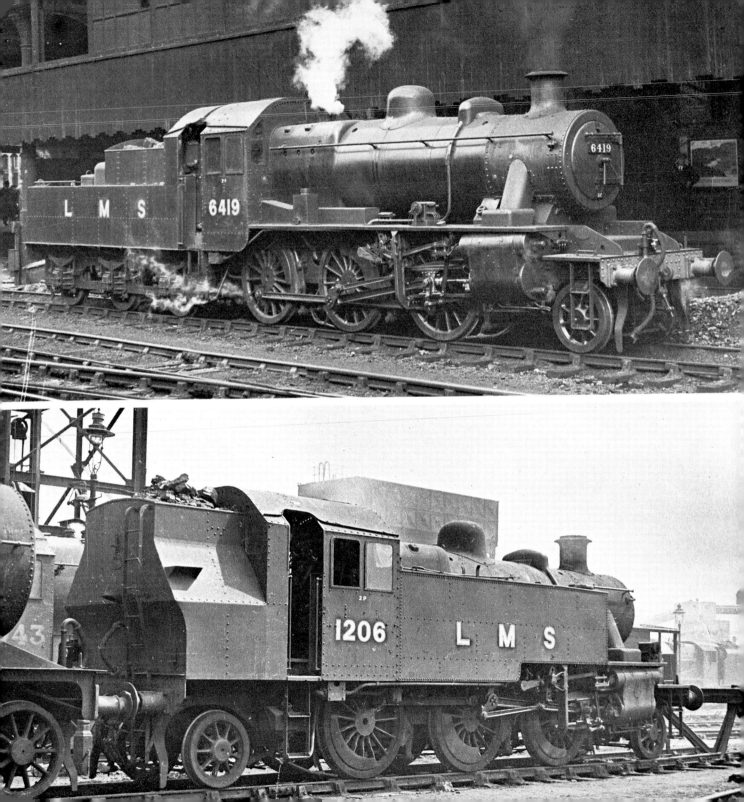

last three new steam locomotive designs for the LMS were brought out by H. G. Ivatt, the final locomotive superintendent
ore Nationalisation, who was in office from 1945–47. Two light Class 2 types for branch and cross-country lines with limited
ght restrictions came out in 1946 almost simultaneously, the 2-6-2T being in fact purely a tank version of the 2-6-0. Both types
e extremely successful; ten of the 2-6-2Ts and twenty of the 2-6-0s appeared under LMS auspices but construction continued
r Nationalisation until there were 130 of the former in traffic and 128 of the latter. The two designs were subsequently adopted
andard for future construction by BR in the form of the 84000 and 78000 classes.

A heavier 2-6-0 Class 4 was the last design of all, of which only the first three, Nos. 3000–3002, which came out at the end of 1947,
appeared as LMS engines. Those which immediately followed had the temporary numbers M3003–M3010, after which the BR
renumbering scheme made the subsequent ones 43011 upwards. This design was also perpetuated by BR in the new 76000 class.
These three illustrations show No. 6419 at Manchester in April 1947, No. 1206 at Derby in July 1947, and No. 3000 at Bletchley in
August 1948. The ugly double chimneys on these engines were later substituted by single blast pipes, with some improvement to
the appearance of what were never particularly good-looking engines.

The LMS was first in the field amongst Britain's railways to explore the possibilities of diesel or diesel-electric locomotives. Initially, consideration was given to whether these might be practicable for yard shunting, mainly to secure the considerable economy which would result from the use of one-man operation. The first experiment consisted in the mounting of a Paxman hydrostatic 400hp engine on the frames of superannuated Midland 0-6-0T No.1831. The new creation, which first appeared in December 1932, retained its old number, and is seen here at Derby in July 1935, along with Class 2 4-4-0 No.459. This was the first straw in the wind which was later to transform the whole picture of the British railway system, and together with electric traction, eventually to oust steam altogether as an instrument of rail propulsion. At the same time that No.1831 was running its trials, orders were placed with outside firms for other experimental machines of varying designs.

Some further examples of LMS pre-war experimental diesel shunters, forerunners of the standard design now seen all over the BR system. No.7055 had a 175hp Mirrlees engine with hydraulic transmission, built by Hudswell Clark in 1934. From 1935 however, 350hp was adopted as the standard power for future construction. No.7064 (above) with jackshaft drive, seen shunting at Carlisle in June 1937, was built by Armstrong Whitworth in 1935, whilst No.7070 came from the works of Hawthorn Leslie in the same year. None of these original LMS engines now remain under BR ownership. Half of them were disposed of to the Ministry of Supply during the war, many going overseas.

95

The LMS was determined to produce Britain's first main line diesel-electric locomotive, and in conjunction with English Electric turned out the 1600hp No.10000 in December 1947, just in time for it to appear as an LMS engine before the railway lost its identity at Nationalisation on 1 January 1948. This machine is seen on the 8.55 a.m. from Derby to St. Pancras approaching Hendon on 23 February 1948. [British Railways, LM Region]